Seatoun of Largo

(A collection of Victorian Photographs
and Largo Today)

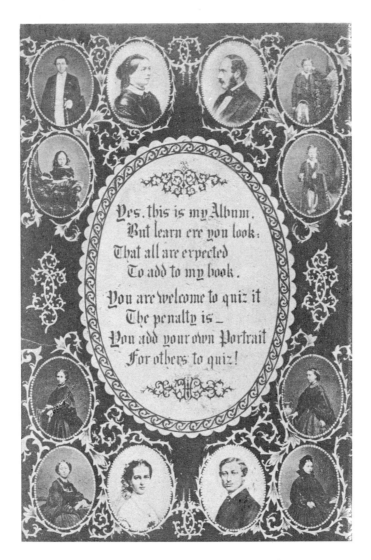

Yes, this is my Album.
But learn ere you look:
That all are expected
To add to my book.

You are welcome to quiz it
The penalty is —
You add your own Portrait
For others to quiz!

H.R.H. Queen Victoria, Prince Albert and family, 1860

Seatoun of Largo

(A collection of Victorian Photographs and Largo Today)

Ivy Jardine

SEATOUN PUBLISHING
ISBN 0 9507803 0 8

W. C. HENDERSON & SON LTD.,
UNIVERSITY PRESS
ST. ANDREWS, FIFE.

For my dear Son

Master David Gillies Jardine

Remembrance for the Past

Good Wishes for the Present

Bright Hopes for the Future

Contents

Acknowledgements for Photographs

For permission to reproduce photographs I am grateful to:

Mrs. E. Band, Lower Largo: A.I.O.

David Gillies, Lower Largo: B.

Freddie Horne, Lower Largo: D.E.

Sir John Gilmour of Montrave: F.G.H.N.

Alan Brotchie, Aberdour: C.

Mrs. White and Mrs. R. Govan, Pittenweem: J.K.L.M.

University of St. Andrews (cover photograph)

Editor of *East Fife Mail*

The Sunday Post, for reproduction of cartoon

For their help, interest and encouragement I am grateful to the following people:

Alan Brotchie, N.B. Traction Group, Dundee

T. Alex. Henderson, Crail, Fife

Sara Stevenson, Edinburgh

Mrs. Isabella Jardine, Upper Largo

William Reid, Lundin Links

Tom Gourdie, Kirkcaldy, for map of Fife and handwriting on cover of book

David and Arnott Wilson, for cover fly-leaf, notes and Latin transcriptions respectively

Ian Copland, District Librarian of North East Fife District Council

John Bates and Margaret Young of Register House, Edinburgh, for cataloguing the Cardy House Archive and all their assistance over the years

My thanks go to:

The Scottish Studios and Engravers for their skill in making the line and half-tone blocks, many of which were taken from faded originals

Mr. R. N. Caddy, W. C. Henderson & Son Ltd., University Press, St. Andrews

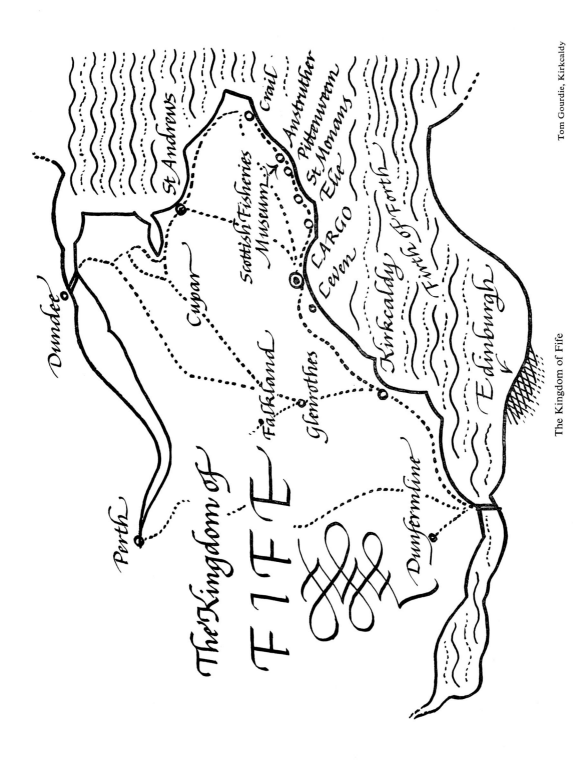

The Kingdom of Fife

Tom Gourdie, Kirkcaldy

9

Introduction

THE NAME of Largo when used in a general sense includes all the villages—Kirkton of Largo or Upper Largo; Seatoun of Largo or Lower Largo; Temple, and Drumochy. My book is concerned mainly with the village of Lower Largo and the Gillies family. Most of the photographs are from the Gillies-Jardine family albums. Since the book contains a large number of photographs I have had to be brief with the written word. I hope therefore to follow this small volume with a book telling of the lives and times of ten generations of one Largo family from 1650 to the present day.

The Rev. R. Brown, the Parish Minister, writing in 1841 pays the people of Largo the following compliment: "There is nothing peculiar in the language or manner of the inhabitants. It argues well for their prudence and management that with wages, as frequently happens, not exceeding six or seven shillings (30/35p) a week, they are able to clothe, educate and feed their families, pay their rent, and defray other necessary expenses. Their general character may be considered as moral and becoming; their kindness to each other in distress is always gratifying to witness; and their attendance at religious meetings, besides the ordinary Sabbath services, is a favourable evidence of their religious character. Religious animosities, which were carried to a disgraceful height, have greatly subsided, and withal, whilst it must be wished that family worship were more cultivated, the 'honouring of all men' more practiced, and their mental resources more employed by the body of the population, still they may be viewed as distinguished by shrewdness and industry, and intelligence, and will no doubt participate in the progressive changes and improvements of the age".

Largo in Victorian times was fairly prosperous compared with many other towns and villages in Scotland, though there were some very poor families in overcrowded houses. James Clunie, Labour M.P. for Dunfermline Burghs, wrote in his autobiography "Labour is my Faith" about the poverty and hardship his family experienced in Lower Largo. He was born in 1889, the youngest of seven children whose father, a fisherman, died when he was eight years old. Mrs. Clunie was left to bring up her seven children alone. The front room of the house was used as a shop by day and sleeping accommodation for some of the children at night. Finally, when James left the village school at 13 years, the whole family left Largo and moved to Dunfermline for jobs in the pits and factories there.

The housing of the village of Lower Largo was varied both in size and situation, the village less than a mile long had back yards but no back streets, the beach providing a natural playground for the children. The population of Lower Largo in 1860 was 570. The Largo railway line and station was opened in 1856.

My book was originally intended for family and friends; however, it has been suggested to me that it might enjoy a wider circulation. I have found great difficulty in selecting the photographs from our families' large collection and to being as brief as possible with the text, there is so much of interest here. However, I have enjoyed getting the book together and hope family and friends will be pleased with the final result.

IVY JARDINE,

Cardy House,
Lower Largo, Fife.
January 1982.

The old Seatoun of Largo, or Lower Largo as it is known today, was once a thriving, bustling place, with its centuries-old rubble pier and a steamboat which plied twice a day in summer and daily in winter between Newhaven and Largo. The harbour which lies at the mouth of the Keil Burn was not accessible at more than half-tide. Passengers from the Steamer were ferried ashore in the "Florry Boat"

11

The "Tattie Boat" above was a frequent visitor to Largo. The local farmers brought their farm carts laden with potatoes down the steep hill to the pier and helped load them on the boat to be later shipped to Germany and the Netherlands.

These Victorian farm carts were made by the Elder family, Lower Largo

Photo: Glass Negative

The Flax Spinning Mill at the harbour opened in 1840 and employed 85 men and women.

The spinners worked a 56 hour week for a weekly wage of 9/- (45p). Some years later cheap continental yarns began arriving in Scotland and as a result of this many spinning mills had to close down. The Largo Mill closed in 1864.

Flax Spinning Mill, from the Railway Bridge

These old buildings have long since disappeared.

Linseed Oil and Cake Mill

13

Largo midwife, Mrs. M. Bethune, kept a written record of all the mothers she attended from 27th February 1853 to 9th February 1887. Her Register of Births show that there were two thousand and thirty-four births in the parish of Largo, with twenty-nine still births and the loss of only one mother, a remarkable achievement.

She was helped occasionally by the Largo doctor, George Lumgair when a difficult birth was expected.

A   Nurse Bethune

Photo: Hanan & Hardie & Federwitz, Kirkcaldy

Dr. George Lumgair and his wife outside their home in the South Feus, Kirkton of Largo, 1870

Largo in the 19th Century was said to be famous for its shells, smells and bairns and its people to be honest, sober and industrious.

Photo: James Gibb, Dundee, 1870

Photo: J. Patrick, Leven, 1860

Photo: Adam Diston, Leven, 1880

In the winter evenings the young people of the parish met in the village school, where they were taught Scottish country dancing by one "Shufflin Katie" who accompanied the dancers on a pocket-size fiddle.

15

A well dressed young Largo man of the 1840's

Daguerrotype Photograph, *c.* 1850

16

In 1854 the crinoline appeared, introduced by the Empress Eugenie, wife of Napoleon III. Hoops of steel, bound together in a variety of ways, and graduated in size like a beehive from the waist downwards, were worn by ladies to keep their skirts off the legs; the gown was exaggerated further by covering the skirt with large flounces, (as many as seven or eight being hung on between the foot and the waist), or even by wearing a double skirt over the flounces. In the fifties, it was said there were no young people, as this fashion was fatal to youth and beauty. Sleeves became narrow at the shoulder and wide at the wrists and were known as 'Pagoda' sleeves. In 1867 the fronts of the dresses assumed straighter lines so that it became possible to make a dress of eleven or twelve yards of cotton or silk instead of sixteen or seventeen. From 1868 skirts gradually grew narrower; the circular crinoline gave place to the bird-cage bustle for the back of the dress. Soon the polonaise was at the height of popularity; it was fashionable to wear two or more colours, the under skirt being of one hue and the polonaise — which was an upper skirt and bodice combined — of another. In 1875 an extreme style called the 'pin back' made its appearance. The front and sides of the skirt were drawn tightly over the legs and what fulness there was appeared at the back in various folds; it was the opposite of the crinoline. Ladies, instead of presenting a balloon-like shape, now tried to see how slim they could make themselves.

Under the Mistletoe
Augustus thinks Crinoline a detestable invention

From *Punch*, January 1857

Largo Faces and Fashions 1850s-70s

Photo: J. Patrick, Leven

Photo: J. Howie, Edinburgh

Photo: J. Patrick, Leven

Photo: J. Patrick, Leven

Photo: D. Horne, Elie

Photo: A. Diston, Leven

18

Photo: J. Macnair, Glasgow

Photo: D. Gordon, Sinclairtown

Photo: A. Diston, Leven

Photo: J. Gibb, Dundee

Photo: D. Gordon, Sinclairtown

Photo: A. Diston, Leven

19

Photo: A. Diston, Leven   *Photo:* A. Diston, Leven   *Photo:* A. Donald, Dundee

Photo: Nimo & Son, Edinburgh   *Photo:* J. Horsburgh, Edinburgh   *Photo:* A. Diston, Leven

20

Lower Largo from Cardy House roof 1890. Most of the houses are built of Whinstone and others of Sandstone

Photo: J. Terras, Markinch

Above, a Largo woman spinning flax on a bobbin-flyer wheel; the wheel could be turned by hand or by foot using the treadle, a later invention which left the hands free and speeded production. The flax is seen here on a distaff.

David Selkirk Gillies at the age of 24 designed and built a net manufactory near his family cottage in Lower Largo. His brothers John, James, Robert and William helped with the woodwork and setting up the Blacksmith's Shop inside the factory. It opened in 1867 and employed about 60 women. David was educated at the village school and completed his education at 13 years of age.

David Selkirk Gillies, 1867
Photo: J. Porter, Anstruther

Below:
During the lunch hour some of the workers played bowls on the Bowling Green laid out in front of the factory, others sat on the beach if the weather was fine.

The workers outside the net factory
Photo: J. Terras, Markinch, 1885

23

Women inside the net factory

Photo: J. Terras, 1885

There were 36 machines, a fairly heavy net was made weighing 13½lbs. plus 60 yds. long. Heavy guarding at the top and bottom of the nets was put on by hand by the "guarders" in their own homes. The nets cost 25/- (£1.25p). The cotton was bought from Robert Thatcher, Oldham, Lancs.

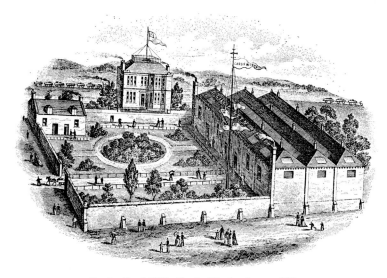

Trade Card 1872, Cardy Works, Largo, Fife

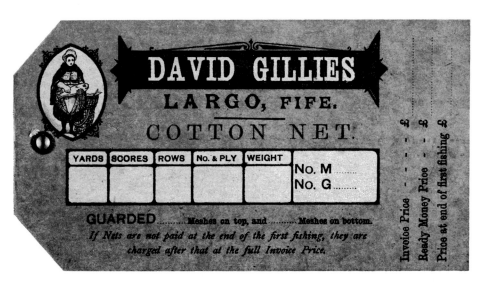

Coloured label for cotton nets

Largo nets were sent out to Melbourne, Australia to James Allan. A cousin of D. Gillies, James, a school teacher, had emigrated from Largo in 1870. He worked for the fishermen in his spare time

TERMS FOR NETS: PER CENT OFF FOR READY CASH ON DELIVERY OF THE NETS, OR   PER CENT OFF AT END OF FIRST FISHING.

NO DISCOUNT ALLOWED IF NOT PAID AT END OF FIRST FISHING, AND AFTER THAT ONE SHILLING PER NET ADDED PER ANNUM.

Letterheading for Cardy Works, 1870

DAVID GILLIES,

NET MANUFACTURER.

CARDY WORKS, **LARGO** FIFE.

PRICE LIST OF BEST QUALITY COTTON NETS, &c.

No. 36/9 Ply.					No. 40/9 Ply.					No. 43/9 Ply.					No. 45 & 50/9 Ply.				
Score	Yds.	About	£	s.	d.	Score	Yds.	About	£	s.	d.	Score	Yds.	About	£	s.	d.	Score	Yds.	About	£	s.	d.
18	50	14 lb.	1	18	9	18	50	12¾lb.	1	17	6	18	50	12 lb.	1	16	6	18	50 10 to 11 lb.	1	15	6
18	54	14¾ ,,	2	1	6	18	54	13½ ,,	2	0	0	18	54	12¾ ,,	1	19	0	18	54 11 to 12 ,,	1	18	0
18	55 14½ to 15 ,,	2	2	6	18	55 13½ to 14 ,,	2	1	0	18	55	13 ,,	2	0	0	18	55 11 to 12 ,,	1	19	0
18	60 15½ to 16 ,,	2	5	6	18	60 14½ to 15 ,,	2	4	0	18	60	14 ,,	2	3	0	18	60 12 to 13 ,,	2	2	0
18	81	22 ,,	3	2	3	18	81	20 ,,	3	0	0	18	81	19 ,,	2	18	6	18	81 16 to 18 ,,	2	17	0
18	100	28 ,,	3	17	6	18	100	26 ,,	3	15	0	18	100	24 ,,	3	13	0	18	100 20 to 22 ,,	3	11	0
20	50	15¼ ,,	2	3	0	20	50	14 ,,	2	1	9	20	50	13 ,,	2	0	6	20	50 11 to 12 ,,	1	19	3
20	54	16¼ ,,	2	6	0	20	54	14¾ ,,	2	4	6	20	54	14 ,,	2	3	6	20	54 12 to 13 ,,	2	2	3
20	55	16½ ,,	2	7	6	20	55	15 ,,	2	5	6	20	55	14¼ ,,	2	4	6	20	55 12½ to 13½ ,,	2	3	3
20	60	17½ ,,	2	10	9	20	60	16 ,,	2	9	0	20	60	15½ ,,	2	8	0	20	60 13½ to 14½ ,,	2	7	0
20	81	24 ,,	3	9	0	20	81	22½ ,,	3	6	9	20	81	21 ,,	3	5	3	20	81 18 to 19½ ,,	3	3	6
20	100	31 ,,	4	6	0	20	100	28 ,,	4	3	6	20	100	26 ,,	4	1	0	20	100 22 to 24 ,,	3	18	6

1/ extra for 36 Rows, and 2/ for 37 Rows. | Finished with Heavy Cotton all round.

TERMS FOR NETS :— 1½ per cent. for Prompt Cash, or   per cent. and   Month's Approved Bill from date of Invoice.

COTTON TWINE.

Mounting and Guarding Sorts,...............1/4 per lb. | Mending Sorts, No. 32, 34, and 36/9 Ply,......1/5 per lb.
No. 40 and 43/9 Ply, ...1/6 ,,

Price List of nets

AMERICAN COTTON CANVAS, 22 inches wide.

No. 1,	2,	3,	4,	5,	6,	7,	8,	9,	10,
1/2,	1/1¼,	1/0½,	11¾d,	11d,	10½d,	10d,	9½d,	9d,	8½d per yard.

ENGLISH COTTON CANVAS, 24 inches wide.

No. 1,	2,	3,	4,	5,	6,	7,	8,	9,	10,	11,	12,
1/5,	1/4¼,	1/3½,	1/2½,	1/1¾,	1/1,	1/0¼,	11½d,	10½d,	9½d,	8½d,	7½d, per yard.

TERMS FOR TWINES AND CANVAS:—2½ per cent. for Prompt Cash.

Dear Sir,

I have pleasure in handing you about my Twines & Prices of Net Cotton Weft, &c. and shall be happy to receive your esteemed orders, which shall at all times have from me my best attention

Your obedient servant,

Price lists sent to the following:- Robert Thatcher, Oldham; Delperre & Co., Boulogne; A. Galbraith, Carradale; Wm. Warburton, Stockport; Peter Kerr & Son, Paisley; Kennedy & Rae, Dundee; Hugh McCormack & Son, Glasgow; W. Paton, Johnstone; I. W. Stewart, Musselburgh; Laycock & Nephew, Manchester; Johnstone; Montrose; Mather & Son, Edinburgh and others

Cardy House

Cardy Works proved very successful and in 1871 D. Gillies designed and built Cardy House. Two travelling Italian artists designed and painted the ornamental plasterwork ceilings. The original Victorian interiors and furnishings have been carefully preserved by the present owner, T. A. Jardine, grandson of D. Gillies.

Cardy Works—net factory from Cardy House front door, 1884

Back of the net factory. The ruin on the right was the old village school which closed in 1868 when a much larger school was built further up the road. Today the boats on the old Bleaching Green have been replaced by the motor car. A few years ago public toilets were built close behind the factory wall.

30

Give a man a fish, you feed him for a day;
Teach a man to fish and you feed him for life.   (*Old Proverb*)

Largo salmon fishers in Largo Bay, 1890

From left: Sandy Simpson, Tam Laurie, David Gillies (Fisher Davie), Bob Melville, John Gillies and Jock Gillies

B

31

THE BOATIE ROWS

Scots Song by James Ewen (1741-1821)

I cuist my line in Largo Bay, and fishes I caught nine,
There's three to sell and three to fry and three to bait the line,
The boatie rows, the boatie rows, the boatie rows indeed;
And happy be the lot of a' that wish the boatie speed.

O weel may the boatie row, that fills a heavy creel
And cleeds us a' frae head to foot and buys our parritch meal.
The boatie rows, the boatie rows, etc.

When Jamie vow'd he would be mine and won frae me my heart,
O muckle lighter grew my creel, he swore we'd never part.
The boatie rows, the boatie rows, the boatie rows fu' weel,
And muckle lighter is the lade when love bears up the creel.
My curtch (cap) I put upon my head and dressed mysel fu' braw,
I trow my heart was dawf (sad) and wae, when Jamies gaed awa'.
But weel may the boatie row, and lucky be her part;
And lightsome be the lassie's care, that yields an honest heart.

When Swanie, Jock and Janetie, are up to gotten lear (learning),
They'll help to gar the boatie row, and lighten a' our care;
The boatie rows, the boatie rows, the boatie rows fu' weel,
And lightsome be her heart that bears, the murlain and the creel;
And when wi' age we are worn doon and hirplin' round the door,
They'll row to keep us dry and warm, as we did them before;
Then weel may the boatie row that wins the bairnies breid,
And happy be the lot of a' that wish the boatie speed.

Life for the Fife fisherman was very hard indeed, exposed often to an extremely cold and variable temperature from sunset until dawn, and often amidst disappointment and loss "toiling all night and catching nothing" with wind, sea and rain beating over him. The fishermen of Fife were known as daring, resolute fellows, their boats almost invariably the most successful when herring fishing at Lowestoft, Berwick-on-Tweed or off the Irish coasts.

In November 1863, when returning from the Norfolk coast, 36 Fife fishing boats were lost in a fearful storm that had started suddenly with little warning.

32

Engraving of a fishwife by the Largo artist and engraver William Ballingall, 1876

The colourful costumes of the fisher lassies were much admired, as were the beautiful jerseys hand-knitted for the fishermen by their wives, mothers and sisters. These patterns were handed down from one generation to another. The fisherwomen required strong limbs and backs to transport the huge willow creels in which they carried the fish to their customers, some walking many miles a day.

The Scottish fisherwomen are the most striking looking people and are generally young and pretty women, very clean and very Dutch looking, with their white caps and bright coloured petticoats. They never marry out of their class. — *From Queen Victoria's Journal, 1842.*

BOAT OWNERS AND SKIPPERS, LARGO 1861

Ballingall, David	Gillies, David (fisher Davie)	Guthrie, Rob
Ballingall, John	Gillies, James	Guthrie, Walter
Ballingall, James	Gillies, John	Lindsay, Rob
Ballingall, Robert	Gillies, Samuel	Melville, Thomas
Butters, James	Gillies, William	Sharp, John
Clunie, John	Gowans, William	Sime, Joseph
Gillies, Alexander		

The morning catch, Lower Largo

c

Largo Bay

O, Largo Bay, how many are thy charms,
Smooth are thy waves and soft thy sheltering arms;
No winds can trouble thee except the west,
To many mariners a place of rest
This SELKIRK found when from Fernandez isle,
Returned to Largo and his native soil.

From *The Bee*, November 28th, 1791

"A! what pleasant visions haunt me
As I gaze upon the sea!
All the old romantic legends,
All my dreams come back to me."

Longfellow

CALLER HERRIN' (Fresh Herring)
by Caroline, Baroness Nairne, 1766-1845

Set to music by the celebrated Neil Gow, the air is hauntingly beautiful and is still a popular song today.

Wha'll buy my caller herrin'?
They're bonnie fish and halesome farin';
Wha'll buy my caller herrin',
New drawn frae the Forth?

When ye were sleepin' on your pillows,
Dream'd ye aught o' our puir fellows,
Darkling as they faced the billows,
A' to fill the woven willows;
    Buy my caller herrin',
    New drawn frae the Forth.

Wha'll buy my caller herrin'?
They're no' brought here without brave daring;
Buy my caller herrin',
Hauld through wind and rain.

Wha'll buy my caller herrin'?
Oh' ye may ca' them vulgar farin',
Wives and mithers maist despairing,
Ca' them lives o' men.
    Wha'll buy my caller herrin',
    New drawn frae the Forth?

As far back as the 12th Century the fishing grounds of Largo were noted. Jocelyn, a monk of Furness Abbey, refers to them in his lives of St. Thenaw and St. Mungo.

The Creek returns of 1881 show that there were 34 boats and 60 fishermen in Largo; however, that year proved to be a most disastrous one for the Scottish fishermen. In the Shetland seas in a single day in July 58 fishermen perished, leaving 33 widows and 88 children. In the autumn of the same year there was an even bigger loss of life. On the 14th October a sudden and violent gale swept over the Berwickshire coast, overtook and overwhelmed the fishing fleet, resulting in the loss of 191 fishermen, who left 107 widows and 351 children. With what terrible significance do the lines of 'Caller Herrin' apply to that fatal year.

Mrs. I. Gillies with Isabella and James, Temple, Lower Largo

The Temple, once a separate village now part of Lower Largo, dates back to medieval times and the Knights of St. John of Jerusalem, a 12th century Religious Military Order; they had lands in many parts of Scotland as well as overseas.

The cottages were known as Burnside Cottages.

OPENING OF LUNDIN LINKS GOLF CLUB HOUSE

Saturday,
April 4th 1896.

Invitation

The original Golf Club was founded in 1868. The new Clubhouse was designed by P. L. Henderson, Edinburgh, an enthusiastic member of the earlier Club which was a modest brick cottage of two rooms.

On the date of the opening of the Clubhouse there were 150 members. The annual subscription was 2/6 (12½p). The membership rapidly increased to 400 by 1907.

Golf match between Forgan and Stewart v. Wull and Bob Gillies. The champion frae the west putts and misses — Oh the language! — Wull putts and halves the match.
(written on back of photograph)

Some of the members of the Lundin Golf Club, 1896

D   'Auld Boab', the Starter at the Lundin Golf Club. The building on the far left is the Victoria Hotel; some years ago it was converted into private flats

E   Sir John Gilmour, Bart., of Lundin and Montrave, seen here addressing the ball with Club members looking on

The Kingdom of Fife's own Regiment, The Fife Light Horse, Commanding Officer in 1895 was Lieut. Col. John Gilmour of Lundin and Montrave. He was created a baronet at Queen Victoria's Diamond Jubilee in 1897. The Regiment was given the new title The Fife and Forfar Regiment was the most popular Regiment in The Fife and Forfar Yeomanry in 1908. It was said by many that The Fife and Forfar Regiment was the most popular Regiment in the British Army.

F

Captain John Gilmour, son of the First Baronet, soldier, politician and farmer. Sir John had a distinguished army and political career, he took an active interest in his farms and did much good work to improve the lot of the Fife farmworkers.

G   *Photo:* W. Stuart, Cupar, 1900

H   Officers and men of the Fife Light Horse leaving for South Africa and the Boer War

Largo Kirk

Photo from a glass negative *c*. 1900

Largo Parish Church; the 17th century spire is a graceful feature of the local landscape.

A history of this historic church, "Largo Kirk", written by the present minister, Rev. Douglas Lister, and the late James Gillies, is available from the minister.

Largo Kirk Session Records 1670-1892 (Ref. CH2/960) are kept in the Scottish Records Office, Register House, Edinburgh.

In Victorian times Largo Parish had five Churches: the Established Church or the Auld Kirk, the Free Kirk, the United Presbyterian Church and two Baptist Churches.

It used to be said that the Free Kirk was the "Wee Kirk", the Kirk without the steeple, while the Auld Kirk was the "Cauld Kirk", the Kirk without the people.

The Kirk spoke out strongly against the evils of strong drink which is not surprising considering that there were four Inns and sixteen licensed Ale Houses in the Parish.

The Rev. David Malloch (*on the right*) was minister of the Largo United Presbyterian Church, Lower Largo from 1860 to 1896. He was a pastor much loved by the congregation, which was mainly fishermen and their families.

A wall plaque to his memory in the church has the inscription:

"For 36 years (he) went out and in among them, speaking words in season to the weary and comforting the afflicted, while his Christian qualities and generous sympathies won for him the esteem and reverence of his flock and of all who knew him."

Photo: T. & R. Annon & Sons, Glasgow

(*Below*)   I
The Largo U.P. Church Choir outing to Glenfarg

45

Ploughing in the shadow of Largo Law

Largo Law, to the north of Largo, can be seen from a great distance. It is 965 feet high; in olden times it was used as a beacon hill to warn the people of approaching dangers. A magnificent view can be seen from its summit on a fine day.

Mr. Murray, blacksmith, repairing a potato digger outside
Pirnwindy Blacksmith Shop, Largo

Farm bairns

Ploughing Matches were organised by the local Agricultural Societies, this encouraged the development of skill in ploughing. There were also harness and good grooming of the horses competitions. Cups, Medals and Silver Spoons were awarded as prizes.

Photographs: James Darling, 1890

Hillhouse Farm, Largo   J

Mr. and Mrs. Arthur had six daughters and two sons. There was no running water in the farmhouse. On the far right is the wash house where the family washed

William Arthur of Hillhouse Farm, Largo, known as "Auld Blowhard", who sold milk in Lower Largo in the 1880's. William blew a whistle and the people came out with their jugs. If the jug was warm he sent them back to rinse it in cold water   K

James Rodger of Branxton Farm, Largo, 1890   L
Photo: Edwin Walker, Dundee

Typical working dress of the East Fife farmworkers. The hats the women are holding were worn in the
fields to protect the head and neck from the sun   *Photo:* Edwin Walker, Dundee, 1890   M

49

Miss Simon with William Blackie, stud groom on Montrave Estate
Photo: Lady Henrietta Gilmour of Montrave

Lady Henrietta Gilmour was probably the first woman in Scotland to take up photography. Fifteen hundred of her glass negatives, dating from 1890-1910 were deposited by her grandson, the present Sir John Gilmour, 3rd Baronet of Lundin and Montrave, in St. Andrews University in 1978.

A keen sportswoman Lady Henrietta had the honour of being made the first lady member of the Royal Caledonian Curling Club.

Lady Henrietta Gilmour of Montrave

The Allan family visiting the Red Lion Hotel, Newton Mearns, Glasgow

And every husbandman, round Largo Law,
    Hath scrap'd his huge-wheel'd dung-cart fair and clean,
Wherein, on sacks stuff'd full of oaten straw,
    Sit the Goodwife, Tam, Katey, Jock, and Jean;
In flow'rs and ribbons drest, the horses draw
    Stoutly their creaking cumbersome machine,
As on his cart-head sits the Goodman proud,
And cheerily cracks his whip and whistles clear and loud.
            From *Anster Fair*, canto second XXV, by Dr. William Tennant

Largo Silver and Brass Band, 1890

There was also a Children's Penny Whistle Band which met in the Templars Hall. Concerts in the Village School were always popular occasions, as was the Largo Choir of 80 voices who performed the works of Mendelssohn and Handel in the Parish Church.

Dr. Samuel Johnson on a visit to St. Andrews in 1773 said, "I did not come to Fife to get a good dinner, but to see savage men, and I have not been disappointed"!

Largo Curlers

Largo Curling Club was admitted to the Royal Caledonian Curling Club in 1841; today the 'Roarin Game' is played mostly indoors. Every few years a Bonspiel takes place when curlers from all over Scotland take part in a 'Grand Match' on a frozen loch.

Largo House   *Photo:* Cowie, Largo 1890

Largo House, designed by John Adam in 1750 for General James Durham of Largo. It commands an extensive view of the Forth and the surrounding country. One of the Durham proprietors is credited with having given Edinburgh its name of "Auld Reekie". Accustomed to seeing the chimney smoke of Edinburgh rising out of the hills in the distance, he timed his household prayers by its rising smoke saying "It's time noo bairns tae tak the buicks and gang tae bed, for yonder's Auld Reekie putting on her night cap".

The General's brother, Admiral Philip Durham, later succeeded to the estate of Largo. Admiral Durham was one of the few survivors of the ship the "Royal George" when she foundered at Spithead in 1782. A canon from the "Royal George" stood on the lawn of Largo House for many years.

Today this once magnificent mansion is now a roofless ruin.

> Here ladies bright were often seen
> Here valiant warrier trod;
>
> .   .   .
>
> But a' are gone the guid the great
> And neathing noo remains,
> But ruin sitten' on the wa's
> And crumblin' doon the stains!
>   H.F.

Alexander Selkirk

ALEXANDER SELKIRK was born in the Seatoun of Largo in 1676. He was the seventh son of John Selcraige and Euphan Mackie. Selkirk's eldest brother David worked with his father in the shoemaker shop in the village, while his other brothers went to sea. Alexander was educated at the village school, where he showed considerable aptitude for mathematics and navigation. He was his mother's favourite son; his mother, we are told, had formed "most extravagant hopes for him".

Like most of the other young men of the village, Selkirk went to sea, not as a fisherman like his brothers, but to join one of the many privateering expeditions against the French and Spanish colonies. Soon his experience at sea and a definite flair for navigation advanced him in rank from common seaman to respected navigator.

In the year 1704 Selkirk joined a privateering expedition under Captains Dampier and Pickering. Selkirk was appointed sailing master of the "Cinque Ports" under Captain Pickering. When Pickering died command passed to Lieutenant Thomas Stradling. Aboard the "Cinque Ports" all was not well. Captain Stradling was a hard and rather mediocre commander. Forty-two of his crew went ashore and declared they would not re-embark so long as Stradling commanded. Later Captain Dampier of the "St. George" persuaded the men to return to their duty, but dissension and bitterness continued to afflict the "Cinque Ports" and Alexander Selkirk shared the lack of confidence the crew felt for its captain. The ship by now was well riddled with shot, the result of more than one "engagement" on the high seas; Selkirk warned the captain that the ship was not safe and that he wished to leave the vessel on the first opportunity. When the ship finally reached Juan Fernandez early in October, he resolved to leave the ship and join the next friendly privateer. Selkirk was landed on the Chilean island of Juan Fernandez 400 miles off Chile's central coast, with his sea chest containing his clothes and bedding, his mathematical instruments and navigation books, his Bible, a kettle, hatchet and his gun. Selkirk's decision to leave his ship was a sound one. After leaving Juan Fernandez, the "Cinque Ports" returned to the Peruvian coast, where it foundered on an island off Babacora. Before sinking, the vessel struck her Colours before a Spanish force. Stradling and seven of his men were saved and spent the next seven years in a Lima prison!

Most of what we know of Selkirk's four years and four months on the island comes from the account of his rescuer another privateer, Captain Woodes Rogers, and Sir Richard Steele, who published a political journal called "The Englishman", and included an account of Selkirk in his Journal in December 1713. After meetings with Selkirk in London, Sir Richard wrote, "I had the pleasure frequently to converse with Selkirk soon after his arrival in England in the year 1711. It was a matter of great curiosity to hear him, as he is a man of good sense, given an account of the different revolutions in his own mind in that long solitude".

When the famous English sea captain, Woodes Rogers, and his pilot, one Captain W. Dampier, the best hydrographer and geographer of his day, arrived off the island of Juan Fernandez in the frigate "Duke" on February 1st 1709, they saw a light ashore and wondered who was on the uninhabited island. The following morning they sent their pinnace ashore to investigate. Woodes Rogers wrote in his journal: "Immediately our pinnace returned from the shore and brought abundance of crayfish with a man cloathed in goat-skins, who looked wilder than the first owners of them. He had been on the island four years and four months, being left there by Captain Stradling of the 'Cinque Ports'; his name was Alexander Selkirk, a Scotsman who had been Master of the 'Cinque Ports', a ship that came here last with Captain Dampier, who told me that Selkirk was the best man on her, and I immediately agreed with him to be a Mate on board our Ship". Woodes Rogers continues: "Selkirk diverted and provided for himself as well as he could; but for the first eight months he had much ado to bear up against melancholy and the terror of being left alone in such a desolate place, but by the favour of providence and vigour of his youth, being now but thirty years old, he came at last to conquer all the inconveniences of his solitude and to be very easy". Woodes Rogers styled Selkirk the Governor of Juan Fernandez. Captain Woodes Rogers was impressed with Selkirk and gave him command of the "Increase", one of the small prizes taken in the South Seas from the Spaniards by the "Duke" and "Duchess".

It was not until October 1711 that Selkirk landed in England. The account of his adventures excited great interest in London, where he frequently met Sir Richard Steele. After getting his share of the prize money, which amounted to £800, he made his way back to the old Seatoun of Largo and his surprised family who after his long absence thought he was dead. He stayed for some time in Largo and he frequently bewailed his return to the world, which could not, as he said, with all its enjoyments, restore to him the tranquillity of his solitude. He loved to wander alone in Keil's Den, about a mile from Largo, and to take solitary boating excursions from Largo Bay out to Kincraig Point. He later said that he was a better man while in his solitude than ever he was before, and feared he would ever be again. By 1720 Selkirk was back at sea again, this time as a Lieutenant of His Majesty's ship "Weymouth". However, on the 3rd of December 1721 his Captain recorded in his logbook that Alexander Selkirk died (probably of yellow fever) and was buried at sea at Cape Coast Castle (West Africa).

Scale model of the Selkirk family house

Scale model of the original Selkirk family house made by David S. Gillies in 1865 before he demolished the old house and built the present buildings, known as the Crusoe buildings. He left a niche high in the wall in front of the house empty until he could afford to put up the statue to Selkirk in 1885.

(Model in Cardy House)

Photo: P. F. Patrick, Edinburgh

THE STATUE IN MEMORY OF ALEXANDER SELKIRK

This stands in the village of Lower Largo and is popularly known as the Crusoe Statue. It is placed high in a niche in front of the house which occupies the site of Alexander Selkirk's birthplace.

It stands over six feet high and shows him as Woodes Rogers records that he appeared to his rescuers, "A man cloathed in goatskins who looked wilder than the first owners of them". He wears a rough coat and ragged breeches of goatskin with laced skin sandals on his feet and a pointed goat-skin cap on his head. His left hand is thrust forward grasping the barrel of his long flintlock gun. His right hand shades his eyes as his steady gaze searches the sea-horizon in hope of a rescuing sail.

Underneath is a bronze tablet with the inscription:

"In memory of Alexander Selkirk, Mariner, the original of Robinson Crusoe, who lived on the Island of Juan Fernandez in complete solitude for four years and four months. He died 1723. Lieutenant of H.M.S. Weymouth. This statue is erected by David Gillies, net manufacturer, on the site of the cottage in which Selkirk was born".

The statue, which is a fine example of the work of T. Stuart Burnett, A.R.S.A., is of bronze and was cast by Sir John Steele, R.A., in his foundry in Leith. It was unveiled by the Countess of Aberdeen on 11th December 1885.

The date of death has since been found to be an error. He died in the roadstead at Cape Coast Castle (West Africa) on 3rd December 1721 and was buried at sea.

(Photograph taken in Edinburgh before the statue was placed in position in Largo.)

Selkirk's Island is about 14 miles in length and 8 miles in width; its height is over three thousand feet; its distance from Chile, to which country it belongs, is four hundred miles.

The land fauna includes herds of wild goats, humming birds, doves and coatis, while the marine fauna is even richer. The hills are well wooded, the valleys fertile, and pouring down through many ravines are streams of pure water.

Memorial tablet to Alexander Selkirk erected on Juan Fernandez Island by Commodore Powell and the Officers of H.M.S. "Topeze" in 1868. It stands high up on the mountain near the place known as "Selkirk's Look-out" about 2800 feet above sea level, where it is possible to see all the island. It was here he used to go each day to look out for a friendly passing ship.

58

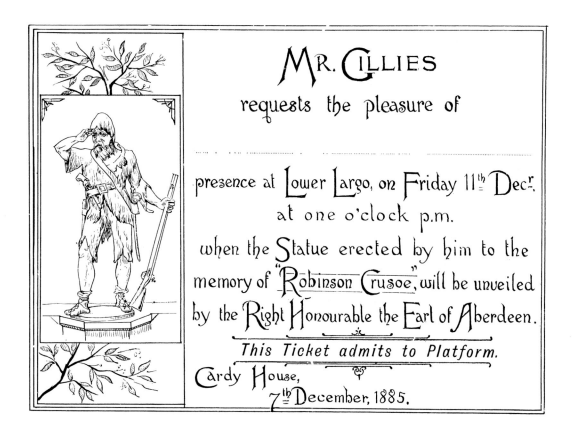

MR. GILLIES

requests the pleasure of

....

presence at Lower Largo, on Friday 11th Decr.
at one o'clock p.m.
when the Statue erected by him to the
memory of "Robinson Crusoe", will be unveiled
by the Right Honourable the Earl of Aberdeen.

This Ticket admits to Platform.

Cardy House,
7th December, 1885.

Dr. Hay Fleming of St. Andrews, who visited the old Seatoun on the day of the unveiling of the Selkirk Statue, wrote that "the 11th December 1885 will ever be a red letter day in the local Calendar. The triumphal arches, the great processions, the Earl of Aberdeen's speeches and the unveiling of the monument by his Countess will never be forgotten".

The *Dundee Courier* reported that over 500 people left Dundee by special train to view the statue, many travelled from distant parts to see it, and that David S. Gillies, to whom the present generation is — as posterity will be — indebted for his commendable public spirit in erecting a memorial to Alexander Selkirk.

The unveiling of the Selkirk Statue, Lower Largo

The *Scotsman* newspaper, 12th December 1885, gives a full account of the celebrations which took place that day, also the names of the platform party and speeches made by some of the guests present

Main Street, Lower Largo, 11th December 1885

Photographs by John Terras, Markinch

Main Street, Lower Largo

A trades procession in which all the industries of the Parish were represented, was followed by the **Largo Silver and Brass Band.**

Main Street, East End

There were six triumphal arches along the main street to the harbour, a liberal display of flags and bunting gave the Village a gay appearance.

The Floral Arch near the Railway Station bore the words "Welcome here the Earl and Countess of Aberdeen" and on the other side was, "Will you no' come back again".

Main Street, Lower Largo

"Weel may the Boatie Row", a song which has a special application to Largo and is still a popular song today.

Left: Main Street, Lower Largo

Below: The harbour, Lower Largo

There was dancing on the beach and in the evening, a display of fireworks.

Alexander Elder, representing Alexander Selkirk and holding Selkirk's gun, led the procession along the Main Street. Photograph taken on Largo beach.

When the shilfa hammered her canty sang,
The gowden screens o' the furze amang,
An' the Law tae its cloven croon linked gay,
A strange ship anchored in Largo Bay.
Noo, wha is this, that he kens sae weel
Hoo the bonnie broo o' the Law tae speil,
Altho' there's that i' the luik o' his e'e,
Bespeaks a man frae a far countrie?

It was Sabbath morn, a' the folk had gane
Tae the kirk whaur the stranger sat his lane.

The Dominie on his desk had rapped
Till a' the stratled cob-webs flapped,
When a puir auld wife cried quaverin' hie—
"Oh, here's my son come hame to me!
His coat is taggit wi' gowd an' green,
An' his face eicht years I ha'e never seen—
But a hunner years they wad coont as nane,
For a mither's hert aye kens her ain!"
The Dominie gloomed—"Is the Sabbath day
A time tae anchor in Largo Bay?"

Then oot spak' Selkirk—"I'' never be
Sae guid as I was i' the lane South Sea!"

"Weel, weel! I winna cast my pearls
Afore——ahem! sick glaikit kerls—
Haud! Skipper Broon hoo daur ye smirk
An' cry 'Cauld airn!' through a' the kirk?"*

The kirk it skailed; an' the folk were fain
Tae welcome Selkirk hame again.
Sae he married a wife and settled doon,
Tae live like the lave in Largo toon;
An' he built a bouir tae gladden his e'e,
Like ane he had left i' the far South Sea.
Instead o' it's wa's o' pimento tree,
Stood the red limbed fir o' his own countrie;
Instead o' the grass that Fernandez grew,
'Twas theekit wi' bent frae the Law's e'e-broo.

But a strange luik waukened within his e'e—
He wasna' at hame i' the auld countrie.

He socht Kiel's Den on the autumn morn
When the haws gleamed red on the leafless thorn,
An' the squirrels loupt up the pillars grey,
O' their beechen hames whaur the nut-hoards lay.
But the things o' the wuds luiked a' askance
At the wanderin' man wi' the restless glance,
Save Robin' alane, sae trig an' wee,
O' the canny fit an' the trustfu' e'e.

He wandered the shores o' the Firth an' saw
The solan hie tae the Bass awa',
An' oot o' his breist wad his heart maist flee
Tae his lanely isle i' the far South Sea
An' he wad climb tae Largo Law
Wi' the mantlin' cluds roon her coif o' snaw,
An' hide i' the morning' mists that curled
Wi' the fisher's prayers tae a higher world.

But aye there lay i' the howe o' his e'e,
The luik o' a man frae a strange countrie.

When winter storms ower the Firth wad whirl,
An' the Bay was loud with the sea-mews skirl,
An' the long blasts soughed frae the norlan' sea,
His thochts tae his island bouir wad flee.
At lang an' last he could nae mair thole,
The waefu' langin that starved his soul;
Sae he bade fareweel tae his mither dear,
An' clasped his wife wi' mony a tear—
For nature's spell it had made him fain
Tae own nae kinship but jist her ain.

An' the sails o' his ship that swung sae free,
Were set fur the shores o' Eternity.

JESSIE PATRICK FINDLAY, Kirkcaldy, *c.* 1900

*The word "swine" was considered unlucky among fisherfolk; and as a counterspell they touched the iron heels of their boots crying "Touch cauld airn!"

The above poem first appeared in "The Fife News Almanac", and was later included in Edwards' "Modern Scottish Poets".

Just three months after the Selkirk Celebrations on the 30th of March 1886 the village was mourning the loss of a Largo fishing boat the "Brothers". She was last seen 50 miles east of the May Island. She had a splendid crew and had weathered many a storm. It is believed that she was swamped by a heavy sea, while the crew were "hauling their lines" with the hatches off.

Samuel Gillies, Skipper of the "Brothers"
Photo: Milliken, Kirkcaldy

Those who lost their lives were:

Samuel Gillies, Skipper, aged 45 years
John Gillies, son, aged 23 years
Alexander Gillies, son, aged 21 years
David Wishart, aged 47 years

David Wishart, son, aged 23 years
James Wishart, son, aged 21 years
John Johnston, aged 23 years

The Kirk kept a Boat Disaster Fund, which was a great help to the widows and children of fishermen lost at sea. (The fund was wound up many years ago.)

Mrs. Gillies, (Catherine Selkirk), 1779-1862

Death — whose stealthy foot has crossed the threshold alike of prince and peasant — has been again among us working his sad stern work. One of his victims, I would mention one — octogenarian — in whom very many have taken an interest, and to whom many in this locality are connected by the tender ties of kindred. Mrs Gillies died suddenly on 1st inst. of this year 1862, and on 3rd inst. a numerous company of friends and relatives showed their respect for her memory by following her remains to their last resting place in the New Cemetery, Upper Largo. This interesting old woman was widely known as the great-grand niece of Alexander Selcraig or Selkirk, the hero of Defoe's charming romance "Robinson Crusoe".

She was proprietress and occupant of the house in which he was born: and guarded, most religiously, his cup and chest, which as interesting relics had descended as heirlooms in the family. Many visitors have been welcomed to that curious antique-looking thatched house by its kind old inmate, and had been permitted to drink, what pleased them, out of the silver-mounted cocoa-nutshell: to pass their hands over the cunning joinings of the "auld cedar kist", to feel the weight of its heavy rounded lid, and to examine the initials and rude carvings of the lonely exile. I may state that Sir Walter Scott, Than whom none more curious and well versed in antique lore, in company with his publisher, Mr Constable, many years ago visited Largo, and inspected these relics as well as the entries in the Parish Register, relative to Alexander Selkirk. So interested were they that the former took the cup with him, and had a new rosewood stand and silver rim put on it, and the latter carried with him the Parish Registers, and had them handsomely bound for preservation. Many, however, who went to see these relics, turned an eye of still livelier interest upon the shrunk form, and wrinkled face of the aged and pleasant spoken female who exhibited them. And, apart from the interest which her connection with Selkirk gave her, there was much in Mrs Gillies to awaken interest and win respect. Brought up in a rough school, she had experienced a life of labour, of "toiling, rejoicing, sorrowing". A fisherman's wife, the mother of thirteen children, she had no easy task to perform. No one, however, heard her complain: and though numerous deaths in the family circle lacerated her heart, she ever maintained the calmness of her spirit. Throughout her whole life her character was one — industrious, cheerful, contented and eminently christian. Moreover, if Napoleon I. was right when he judged the first woman in his empire to be she who had born most children, surely Mrs Gillies was worthy of honour — in as much as, besides her own respectable family of children, she lived to number about 100 grand children and great-grand children. Add to this the fact of her having trained her household well — of having, as it were, stamped them with her own character — and we must pronounce her worthy of double honour. This mother of a goodly race died at the ripe age of 83.

Her last end was peace:—

"Night dews fell not more gently to the ground
Nor weary, worn out winds expired so soft."

(The Alexander Selkirk Cup and Sea Chest are preserved in the National Museum of Antiquities of Scotland, Edinburgh. His powder horn and clasp knife are kept in Kirkcaldy Museum, Fife.)

James Gillies, 1816-1902

James Gillies, a son of Catherine Selkirk or Gillies, married, nine children, was a ship's carpenter on a whaling ship.

James, like other Largo men, knew the horrors of an Arctic winter when ships crews could be trapped in the ice for weeks and even months at a time, till often the body gave out, frozen, snow-blinded, scurvy-ridden, and starved — to death. The men were exposed to the dangers of ice, the climate, and from the whales themselves. However, they had a certain grim cheeriness and when caught in the ice often made the best of their situation.

An amusing story was told by Captain James Fairweather in 1875; he was mate of the Dundee whaling ship *Victor*. In the Davis Straits the crews of the Dundee fleet went what their captains called "fitba' mad". Footballs were made out of seal skin and whenever a number of ships were in company the ice became covered with energetic players. On one occasion the men were playing football in thick fog, near enough the ship to hear the ship's bell, when suddenly the cry went up, "a bear! a bear!" It appears that in the midst of the game it was suddenly noticed that a full-grown polar bear had joined in and was chasing the ball as eagerly as the keenest footballer. He had emerged unnoticed out of the fog. One can imagine the panic of the men as they rushed to the only ladder hanging over the side of the ship, a swinging rope ladder which the frightened men fought to get a hold. The bear was last seen tearing up the seal skin football.

In spite of the never ending work, the many hardships and the bitter cold, most sailors who had been to the Arctic were pleased to go back again. There was a fascination about the life which, for those who had never experienced it, was hard to realise.

(James Gillies's sea chest and tools can be seen in Kirkcaldy Museum. His descendents have his family bible and other items in Cardy House.)

David Selkirk Gillies, 1843-1923

Photo: J. Terras, 1885

David S. Gillies, eldest son of James Gillies. Married, two children. Founded the Net Manufactory in Lower Largo and erected the Selkirk Statue in 1885. Acted as legal advisor to the people of Lower Largo and kept the community's records for preservation.

Gillies family, 1896
Left: Mrs. D. Gillies with baby James, James (whaler), David S. Gillies and daughter Isabella

Family Tree from 1657-1981. (abbreviated)
John Selcraige—Ephan Mackie, married Largo 1657 (seven sons)

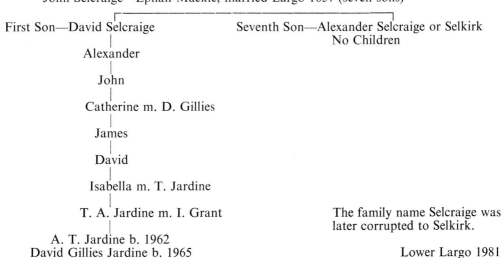

First Son—David Selcraige   Seventh Son—Alexander Selcraige or Selkirk
                                                              No Children
Alexander

John

Catherine m. D. Gillies

James

David

Isabella m. T. Jardine

T. A. Jardine m. I. Grant   The family name Selcraige was
                                             later corrupted to Selkirk.
A. T. Jardine b. 1962
David Gillies Jardine b. 1965   Lower Largo 1981

The yacht Semiquaver was designed and built by the brothers W. and R. Gillies in their little workshop in Lower Largo in 1885. The brothers won many prizes in races throughout Scotland, the local newspaper reported that the yacht "Semiquaver" was a perfect swallow on the waters. The Gillies brothers seamanship was equal to the qualities of their creation, there was nothing to touch her on the Forth.

An earlier yacht was called the "Quaver", on her starboard bow she had painted a few bars of the popular Song "Rocked in the Cradle of the Deep" while on the portside were the opening bars of "The Boatie Rows". The brothers had a great love of music and made their own violins.

The "Semiquaver" in Largo Bay with Largo Law in the background

William and Robert Gillies
Photo: Henry Dyas, Leven, 1886

Drying the sails of the
"Semiquaver" on the
Bowling Green in front of
their brother David's net
factory.

The launching of the "Semiquaver" each summer
always attracted a big crowd
of residents and holiday-
makers.

In 1886 the net factory closed down due to the lack of orders for fishing nets and sail cloth.

The once plentiful herring had deserted the waters and many of the fishermen left the sea to seek jobs elsewhere, or emigrate. For over 100 years now families have been emigrating to all parts of the world from Largo. Today their descendants visit Largo or write for information about the families they are descended from.

Many Largo families who emigrated often left behind the oldest members of their family who wished to remain in Largo. Once settled in the country of their choice they would write to David Gillies and if necessary send money to him for their grandparents' welfare; he arranged to have a nurse or help in the house if needed and saw to it that when the time came they were buried in Largo Cemetery. Mr. Gillies then sold the house and contents on behalf of the family and with instructions from them to send out the family Bible and a "wee minding" of their old home, he usually shipped out the grandfather clock!

(Professor Gordon Donaldson's excellent book, "The Scots Overseas" (1966) tells the story of Scottish emigration.)

Miss D. Stewart

Photo: Zweifel, Duluth, Minn., U.S.A.

From left: Mrs. Forgan, her granddaughter Mrs. C. Stewart, little Adele Stewart, her great granddaughter, and Mrs. David Anderson, her daughter

Photo: J. Terras, 1896

The Stewart family from Duluth, Minn., U.S.A., on a visit home for the hundredth birthday of Mrs. Forgan, Lundin Mill, Lower Largo.

Photographs and postcards were sent back home to Largo with news and views of the emigrants new country.

David Gillies was also involved in shipping, being the major shareholder in the Steam Ship "Largo Bay", the S.S. "St. Andrews Bay", the S.S. "Aberlady Bay", the S.S. "Wick Bay", the Steel Sailing Ship "Buckingham" of Liverpool.

S.S. "Largo Bay" of North Shields (2,046 Tons Register) unloading a cargo of coals from Cardiff, 1881

The Docks, Aden 1881

Ship's crew of the S.S. "Largo Bay", Brooklyn, New York, 27th July 1892
Commander Donald McGregor from Pittenweem (centre; other members of the crew were from the East Neuk of Fife and North Shields

A member of the ship's crew with one of the pilgrims

The S.S. "Largo Bay" picked up pilgrims in Aden and took them as far as Karrachee, 1881.

S. S. "Largo Bay"

SECOND VOYAGE—From Cardiff to Aden with a Cargo of coals; thence to Kurrachee with Pilgrams and loading then a Cargo of wheat &c for Antwerp; thence to the Tyne in Ballast

Left Cardiff 12th November 1881	Arrived at Aden 8th December
,, Aden 14th December	,, at Kurrachee 22nd ,,
,, Kurrachee 2nd Jany. 1882	,, at Antwerp 12th Feby.
,, Left Antwerp 24th Feby.	,, at Shield 25th ,,

Dr.

			£	s.	d.
1881					
Novem. 12	To Disbursments @ Cardiff including Stores &c & 551 12/20 ton Coals at 11/-		910	15	11
28	To—Do—@ Portsaid (Canal dues)		654	10	11
Decem. 8	To—Do—@ Aden, including Expenses taking in Pilgrims		213	15	11
1882					
Jany. 2	To—Do—@ Kurrachee including Address Commission & Brokerage on homeward Charter		770	5	2
9	To—Do—@ Aden, including 80 tons Coals @ 36/-		165	9	6
23	To—Do—@ Portsaid including Canal Dues, Hire of Pilot Steamer in Canal and 154 tons of Coals @ 27/-		1026	15	2
Feby. 4	To—Do—@ Gibraltar including 170 tons of Coals at 21/6		196	7	5
24	To—Do—@ Antwerp		301	2	3
25	To—Do—@ Shields		3	5	,,
	To Wages		503	11	,,
	To Provisions		232	10	2
	To Management for 6 months		100	,,	,,

Cr.

		£	s.	d.
1881				
Novem. 17	By Balance from 1st Voyage	4	18	2
	Cardiff to Aden			
	By Frighton 1815½ tons of Coals @ 14/-	1270	17	,,
	Aden to Kurrachee			
	By Frighton Pilgrims	816	8	1
	Kurrachee to Antwerp			
	By Fright as per Manifest	6073	5	7
	By Brokerage &c Rtd.	269	3	4
	By Shipping Fees	2	11	,,

From David Gillies's Shipping Accounts Book

81

Engineers and firemen of the "Buckingham"

MURDER OF THE CAPTAIN OF THE STEEL SAILING SHIP THE "BUCKINGHAM" OF LIVERPOOL

On the 9th October 1890 the "Buckingham" of Liverpool sailed from Dundee. During the voyage the ship's Captain, Peter Lyall, aged 39 years, from Anstruther, Fife, was murdered by one of the ship's crew. The murderer was one B. Jassiwarra, a native of Calcutta.

The ship was off the Orkney Islands at the time of the murder, and as there was a stiff S.W. gale blowing all the men were aloft shortening sail and no one saw or heard anything.

Jassiwarra had been taken on in Calcutta as assistant cabin steward, and when the "Buckingham" arrived in Dundee on 11th September 1890 Captain Lyall had wanted to dismiss him, but the owners of the "Buckingham" requested the Captain to take him back to Calcutta as they were obliged to return him. Captain Lyall reluctantly agreed to this. The Captain left a wife of six months, who later had their son.

Steel sailing ship "Buckingham" of Liverpool (2,613 Tons Register)

_ Steel Sailing Ship "Buckingham" of Liverpool _

Third Voyage From Dundee to New York on Ballast and loading there a Cargo of
Case Oil for Calcutta and from there with a Cargo of Wheat & Linseed
to Hull, thence to London to load a general Cargo for Australia

Sailed from Dundee 9th October 1890   Arrived at New York 8th Decem. 1890.
— " from New York   — " at Calcutta 20 April 1891.
— " from Calcutta 23 June 1891   — " at Hull 19 Novm. 1891

From October December 26th	To Charges, including Stationary Postage Telegrams	126	2		By Balance fm. last Voyage	1160	14	3
	To Income Tax	143	7	New York to Calcutta			
	To Comn. Brokerage &c paid to Agents & Brokers	460	3	3	By Frt. for Case Oil 2nd terms	4557	10
	To Management Comn.	467	4	7	Calcutta to Hull		
	To Interest	22	5	1	By Frt. for Wheat & Linseed @ 40/ p ton	4872	8
	To Disbursements at Dundee New York, Calcutta, & Hull Stores Wages Provisions &c	4948	2	7			
	To Insurance	1475	9	10			
	To Last Voyage Balance	1160	14	3			
	To Profit on this Voyage	4932	4	2			
June July	To Interim dividend 45% To Dividend of 20% p ann	6093	3	5			

From Statement of Shipping Accounts Book written by D. Gillies

Third voyage of the "Buckingham", 1890. There is no mention here of the murder which took place on this voyage. Captain Lyall was a personal friend of D. Gillies, and a frequent visitor to Largo.

Rt. Hon. H. H. Asquith, M.P.

Above: signed photograph of Rt. Hon. H. H. Asquith presented to William Gillies, Lower Largo, in 1886.

The Rt. Hon. Herbert H. Asquith was elected Liberal Member of Parliament for the East Fife Constituency in 1886. He became Prime Minister in 1908. Mr. Asquith was a respected and popular M.P. in the Largo area. His agent in Largo, Mr. W. Gillies, J.P. (Semiquaver) kept him informed of meetings and other events in the Parish of Largo when Asquith had to be in London for long periods of time.

Mr. Asquith represented East Fife for 32 years; however, in the 1918 Election he lost his seat to his Conservative opponent. In his 'Memories & Reflections', Vol. II, Asquith wrote, "I confess that I felt so little apprehension for my seat that I spent most of my time during the Election in visiting and addressing other constituencies."

have written to Mr Bruce
on the subject, and sent
him a contribution to
the fund which I am
glad to see is going to
be raised

Believe me,
Yours very faithfully,
H. H. Asquith
Mr W. Gillies

Part of Mr. Asquith's letter
Below: Letter in full

20 Cavendish Square W.
6 March 1896.

Dear Mr Gillies,

I am much obliged, by your letter of the 4th, enclosing resolutions passed by the Largo Liberal Association on Feb. 25th.

I am glad to find that upon all the points named in the resolutions I am in complete agreement with the Liberals of Largo, and I shall do all in my power to give effect in Parliament and elsewhere to the views which we hold in common.

I was much distressed to hear of the sad catastrophe to which you refer at the close of your letter. I have written to Mr Bruce on the subject, and sent him a contribution to the fund which I am glad to see is going to be raised.

Believe me,
Yours very faithfully,
H. H. Asquith

The sad catastrophe to which Mr. Asquith refers was the loss of a Largo fishing boat in 1896 when three Largo fishermen drowned in Largo Bay within sight of their own homes. Those drowned were David Melville, Tom Melville and Tom Ballingall.

Photo: J. Moffat, Edinburgh

Rt. Hon. W. E. Gladstone and friends

Marquis of Tweedale   Hon. Mr. Lyttleton   Miss Gladstone   Countess of Roseberry   J. E. Boehm, Esq., A.R.A.
Earl of Aberdeen   Mr. Lacaita
Marchioness of Tweedale   Countess of Aberdeen   Lady Reay
Lord Reay   Robert Jardine, Esq.   Mrs. Gladstone   Rt. Hon. W. E. Gladstone   Hon. W. P. Adam
Lord Wm. Douglas   Earl of Roseberry

The Right Hon. William Ewart Gladstone was Prime Minister in the years 1868, 80, 86 and 92.

Many of the residents of Largo and the East Neuk of Fife travelled by special train to hear him speak in his Midlothian Campaign in the Autumn of 1879.

Mr. Gladstone was proud of his Scottish ancestry. At the Parliamentary Reform Union in the Glasgow Trades Hall in 1865 he said, "The memory of the parents to whom I owe my being combined with various other considerations, make me glad and thankful to remember that the blood which runs in my veins is exclusively Scottish."

The Rt. Hon. W. E. Gladstone and family

The Gladstone photographs are from David Gillies's photograph albums 1860-90.

A member of the Gillies family photographed on her hundredth birthday

Many members of this family have lived to a ripe old age. Living in Largo today are some of their decendants who are well up in their seventies and eighties.

22nd October
1881

A meeting of the Lower Largo
Feuars was held this date
Present- David Gillies
James Gillies
John Gillies
John Clunie
James Guthrie
Of John Gillies in the Chair -
The minutes of last meeting were read &
approved
- The Treasurers accounts for the past
two Years were examined & found Correct
It was agreed to repair the drain leading from
Jean Macks Well as also to give the Latch a
repair
- It was agreed to charge those not having Herring
Boats one shilling for hauling their yauls up
on the green -
John Gillies was elected Chairman &
David Gillies Treasurer for next year with
power to look after the affairs of the
Village & the property   John Gillies
of the Feuars -   Chairman

From the Lower Largo Feuars Book, written by David S. Gillies, Cardy House, 1881

Photo: Adam, Diston, 1886

In the Statistical Account of Fife, 1841, the Rev. R. Brown writing about Largo Parish said: "The people are alive to the benefits of education; there are few children of six years who have not been sent to school and few above sixteen who cannot read and though the distance for some is 2 and 3 miles, this does not prevent attendance". The school subjects taught were reading, writing, arithmetic, latin, book-keeping and navigation. There was also a Subscription Library with 500 volumes.

Miss Raich and pupils, Durham School, Lower Largo
Photo: Lothian & Co., Longtown

Mr. T. Nicol and pupils, Kirkton School, Upper Largo
Photo: D. & W. Prophet, Dundee

The first car in Largo—Mr. Walter Horne with young son Freddie

Walter Horne built the fine houses known as Horne's Buildings, Lower Largo

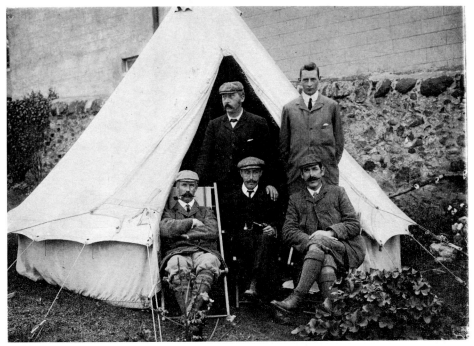

Above, the Committee members of the Largo Field Naturalists Society, founded in 1863. Its members kept a watchful eye on conservation and preservation in the Parish

The Beach, Lower Largo, 1896

John White, Largo, who became Chief Constable of Clackmananshire (Uncle of David Gillies).

Photo: Horsbrough, Edinburgh

The Rev. Dr. David Arnott, 1803-77. One of eleven children he attended the Largo Village School, Edinburgh and St. Andrews Universities. Minister of St. Giles Cathedral, Edinburgh in 1868. (Uncle of Mrs. David Gillies).

Photo: A. Diston

Late Victorian Fashions

Miss Mysie Robertson
Photo: J. Davidson, Edinburgh

Master Jamie Stuart

Photo: Auty, Tynemouth

MacKenzie family, Largo, 1896

Taking tea out of doors was a popular pastime with many Victorian families. The weather must have been better then!

After the Kirk, a walk over the links

Studio photograph with a painted backdrop of the Forth Railway Bridge

Photo: Claude Low, Aberdour

The Jardine family, Kirkton of Largo, Home Farm. The little boy was later badly wounded in the Great War, but recovered and married Isabella Gillies, seen below, aged 2 years.

Photo: T. Wallace, Dalkeith, 1894

Isabella Gillies (Daisy), daughter of David S. Gillies, now a talented musician, artist, and a much loved mother and grandmother to-day.

Photo: J. Terras, 1896

Photo: J. W. McKean, Leith

Photo: A. & G. Taylor, Edinburgh

101

Photo: J. Whyte, Glasgow

Photo: W. K. Munro, Edinburgh

102

James Gillies, 1898

Photo: J. Gay, Pittenweem

Young people outside the Free Kirk, Upper Largo, 1890
The church was replaced by a garage many years ago

Photo: Noble & Son, Hamilton

Photo: J. White, Glasgow

Mrs. David Gillies, Isabella and James, front door of Cardy House, 1898

Photo: W. K. Munro, Edinburgh

Photo: J. W. McKean, Leith

The evening gathering of cronies, Lower Largo, when the men gladly,
"Laid aside all private cares
To mind the Kirk and State affairs"

Contrast in hat styles — Residents of the old Seatoun
beside Cardy House Wall 1890

Photo: J. Terras

107

Into the Edwardian Age

Photographs: Bramwell and Ferguson, Leven

Miss Daisy Gillies, Lower Largo

Miss. I. Dunn, Largo   *Photo:* A. Swan Watson, Edinburgh

109

T. Jardine and his 'soor milk cairt'

The Jardine family sold milk, butter and eggs in the Largo area for over 70 years until 1975. The family won many cups and prizes for their Pedigree Fresian Herd.

Above, the same young man three years later after the hell and horror of the trenches in France during the Great War.

The history of the Scottish Regiments bristles with daring deeds and heroism of the highest order.

Search the past for what is good, and noble,
And create the future from it.

From D. Paul Krugar's last testament

The Present has its Pleasures,
A future hope I know,
Yet prize thy buried Treasures,
Oh! dear past long ago.

Victorian Song, Reyloff

Time Present and Time Past
Are both perhaps present in time future,
And time future contained in time past.

T. S. Eliot

Aerial view of Lower Largo, 1970

Photo: Robb and Campbell Harper Studios, Ltd., Edinburgh

Largo Today

Today the old Seatoun has retained much of its old world charm, still a flourishing village, though the fishing industry has gone and most people now travel out of Largo each day to work in Cupar, St. Andrews, Leven and Glenrothes. In December 1978, the North East Fife District Council designated Lower Largo, from Drumochy to the Temple, a conservation area in recognition of its special architectural and historic interest. The Council pays particular attention to the design of new development to ensure that it is in keeping with the character of the area and encourages the sensitive renovation of existing buildings. Permission is needed for the demolition of buildings and for the felling of trees. The population at present is 890. The younger children attend the village Primary School, Lundin Mill, until the age of 12 years, when they go by school bus to Kirkland High School, Methil. There they are joined by pupils from the Leven, Methil and Buckhaven area. Kirkland High School is a large modern well-equipped Comprehensive School with an excellent remedial department.

In the summer many of the children play golf or go sailing, while others go camping with the Scouts and Girl Guides. The ladies of St. David's Church Woman's Guild organise concerts and coffee evenings for local residents and holidaymakers throughout the summer months. In the winter evenings there are indoor Bowling and Curling Clubs, a local Drama Club and the Largo branch of the Scottish Women's Rural Institute. Highland and ballet dancing is popular with many of the children; their teacher, Ida Ballingall, has had a lot of successful pupils over the years.

There are many attractions near Largo which are popular with Largo folk, for example the Fife Institute of Physical & Recreational Education, Glenrothes, run by the Fife Regional Council Education Committee. Fife Opera, run by the Arts in Fife, is also highly popular.

Our local weekly newspaper, the "East Fife Mail", includes reports and photographs from all the villages in East Fife, together with historical articles and old photographs of the area, a popular nature page for the children and, of course, some national news and sport as well.

The Jurecki family of Largo and Lundin Links are caterers of distinction and many of the local ladies help with functions throughout Scotland on a large and small scale.

The village has two churches — St. David's Church of Scotland (Rev. J. MacKenzie) and the Baptist Church (Rev. J. Campbell)
The Crusoe Hotel
The Railway Inn
The Law Restaurant
Man Friday Cafe
Ice Cream and Fish & Chip Shop, owned and run by the Forte family for the past 60 years
A General Store and Fruit Shop
Two Fresh Fish Shops
A Sub Post Office
Newsagent and Toy Shop
Largo Pottery and Shop
Gillies Art Studios (Workshop and Gallery)
Loom Shop Gallery
Largo Bay Sailing Club
The Durham Hall
Two Car Parks

The Parish of Largo is rich in antiquities. A few years ago Bronze Age "cists" of 1500 B.C. were discovered at Strathairlie.

Largo has always been a popular holiday centre with its many attractions for young and old alike. The residents are always delighted to meet again the holidaymakers who come back year after year and those coming to Largo for the first time.

To my fellow residents I quote a few lines from one of Robert Burns's poems:

> Hear, Land o' Cakes and brither Scots,
> Frae Maidenkirk to Johnny Groats;
> If there's a hole in a' your coats,
> I rede you tent it:
> A chiel's amang you taking notes,
> And, faith, he'll prent it!

Lord Lieutenant of Fife: Sir John E. Gilmour, Bart., D.S.O., of Lundin and Montrave.
Member of Parliament for North East Fife: Mr. Barry Henderson.
Largo District Councillor: Major Bruce Foote.

Crusoe Buildings, Main Street, Lower Largo   *Photo:* G. W. Harvey, Leven

114

Lower Largo from Largo Bay   *Photo:* Talbot Studio, Leven, 1980

The Temple and cark park from Cardy House roof   *Photo:* Talbot Studio, Leven

Donald MacNicol and Peter Rodger of Lower Largo showing a sample of the many fine vegetables and flowers grown in Largo today

("The youth of a nation are the trustees of posterity"—*Disraeli*)

Largo children taking part in a sponsored charity race up Largo Law

Photo: East Fife Mail

The Archer family gutting fish in their fish shop and shed in Lower Largo; note the wee lad with a Victorian arm creel

Photo: Talbot Studio, 1980

Largo Parish War Memorial   *Photo:* G. W. Harvey, Leven

The Memorial stands at the crossroads between Upper Largo, Lower Largo and Lundin Links. It is in the form of a Celtic Cross and was designed by Sir Robert Lorimer, A.R.A., R.S.A. Sir Robert was the architect of the magnificent Scottish National War Memorial in Edinburgh Castle. There are 53 names of the fallen of the Great War 1914-18; included is the name of Lt.-Colonel W. H. Anderson of the H.L.I. Regiment, who was awarded the Victoria Cross, son of the Laird of Strathairly, who lost all four of his sons in the Great War. There are 16 names of those who gave their lives in World War II 1939-45.

The harbour, Lower Largo, has changed little since Victorian times. The old granary is now the Crusoe Hotel.

Photo: G. W. Harvey, Leven

Some of the members of the Largo Bay Sailing Club
From left: Russell Bowers, Roy Walker, Douglas Bowers. Mr. A. Bowers inside the rescue boat, with David Jardine and Mr. John Wilson, Safety Officer, looking on.

Photo: Talbot Studio, Leven, April 1980

Largo Bay Sailing Club is a family Club, where a dedicated Committee train young boys and girls in the art of dinghy sailing, rescue work, etc., with film shows, lectures and fund raising events in the winter evenings. There are Sailing Regattas throughout the summer months and many members take part in competitions at other Sailing Clubs with great success.

Winners of the "Semiquaver" Shield for 1980
Duncan Orkney and his son Colin, with Club Commodore George Ballingall and his wife.
Back row: Club Prize-winners for 1980

Photo: East Fife Mail, 1980

Largo Annual Burns Supper

Poosie Nancy (Ivy Jardine) presenting the haggis to Chairman Graeme Stephens. Looking on are Alistair Grant, T. Allan Jardine and Piper Allan T. Jardine. (The 'Mutch' cap and paisley shawl worn by Poosie Nancy belonged to a member of the Gillies famliy).

Photo: East Fife Mail, 1975

122

Braehead Cottages and Cardy House

The path between the houses is known as the Serpentine and connects Lower Largo with Upper Largo. The path at Cardy House gate leads to the Temple, Lower Largo.

Photo: Talbot Studio, 1980

Photo: Talbot Studio

The Gillies Studio, Main Street, Lower Largo, was in the early 18th Century a group of weavers' cottages. In the 19th Century the buildings were converted to become the workshop of the brothers W. & R. Gillies. It was here that the famous yacht "Semiquaver" was built. In 1966 their nephew, the late James Gillies, restored and converted the building to form an Art Studio and Gallery for local artists and in turn his nephew, T. A. Jardine, the present owner, encourages young local artists and craftsmen to work and exhibit in it.

The popular Lower Largo artist, Martyn Anderson, organises the Studio and Gallery; he can be seen at work in the Studio most days of the week.

Opposite the Gillies Studio is the well-known Loomshop Gallery. Here one can see paintings by many members of the Royal Scottish Academy, Edinburgh.

124

Photo: Talbot Studio

Above: the Selkirk Room, inside the Gillies Studio; here silversmith Lindsay Ballingall, and Hugh Shepherd, craftsman in wood, have their workshop.

The building has been carefully preserved; the door and window openings are original, as are the two fireplaces in the east gable (1740) and still in use today. The pine panelling around this room was brought from an old local church which was being "dung doon". The grandfather clock in the corner belonged to Catherine Selkirk or Gillies, and the model of the Zulu King above the fireplace was made by her son James Gillies, ship's carpenter on a whaling ship.

Anne Lightwood, Lower Largo

Photo: Talbot Studio, 1980

Largo Pottery is a small workshop producing a variety of individual domestic stoneware, garden planters and containers for flowers. It was started in 1972 by Mrs. Anne Lightwood and has recently moved to a new workshop reconstructed from a row of old cottages in the centre of the village. Here visitors may see all processes in the making of pottery from preparing clay through throwing, turning, glazing and finally firing in a gas fired kiln. Although only one or two people work there all pots are hand thrown and finished, and several hundred are completed in a week. These are either sold in the pottery shop or supplied to other craft shops throughout Scotland, and many have found their way abroad to all parts of the world.

Lower Largo Pottery   *Photo:* Talbot Studio, 1980

The well at the top of the photograph was one of many public wells in the old Seatoun. Water was laid on in 1896

James Gillies, Lovat Scouts, 1916   James Gillies, R.N.V.R., 1942

James Gillies, F.S.A., Scot.

The late James Gillies was the son of David S. Gillies; like his father before him, he did a lot of good work for Largo and its people. James's special interest lay in preserving and restoring old buildings in Largo. He designed and rebuilt many of Largo's oldest cottages which had fallen into disrepair; he worked with local tradesmen who had learned the skills from their fathers. James served in the Great War, first with the Lovat Scouts and later as a gunner in the Machine Gun Company. In World War II he served as a naval officer in the R.N.V.R. His letters from the two World Wars are treasured by his family today.

His kindness will be long and gratefully remembered by many in the Parish. Gillies Court, Upper Largo, was named after him by his nephew, T. A. Jardine.

T. A. Jardine cleaning the family Statue

Photo: G. W. Harvey, Leven

Still a big attraction today, the Crusoe Statue draws tourists and others to see and photograph it. Recently television people from New Zealand and West Germany made a film in Largo and Juan Fernandez, Chile, about Alexander Selkirk and his brother David's descendants still living in Lower Largo. Many of David's descendants are scattered throughout the world.

The Crusoe buildings where the statue stands are on the site of the original house in which Selkirk was born. The title deeds and Latin charter show that Selkirk's parents and brother David bought the house in 1676. T. A. Jardine is the present owner of the Statue and buildings, and is the grandson of David S. Gillies.

Photo: G. W. Harvey, Leven, 1976

Chilean visitors to the Tercentenary Exhibition of Alexander Selkirk 1676-1976. Mrs. Carlos Valderamma and daughter with local boys David Jardine and James Finlay. His Excellency the Chilean Ambassador, Rear Admiral Kaare Olsen, and family came up from London to visit the Exhibition, which was organised by the Jardine family, Cardy House, Lower Largo.

Reproduced from "The Sunday Post"

130

The net factory from Cardy House roof, 1980

The Net Factory above never reopened after it closed down in 1886. It was a billet during the Great War for soldiers of the Highland Cyclist Battalion and in World War II was used as a warehouse for storing sugar and other items of food which were on ration at that time. There is no electricity; the original oil lamps remain along the ceiling. The blacksmith shop is still intact, as are the offices and toilets. Note the bowling green in front of the factory where the workers used to play bowls at lunch time. Young David and his friends now play with the same bowls on the green when the weather is fine.

It is hoped that the net factory can open again either as a museum or to provide much needed jobs for young people in the Largo area.

David Gillies Jardine, Great Grandson of David S. Gillies is seen here with the scale model of the Selkirk family house made by his Great Grandfather in 1865.

For David

CREEP BEFORE YOU GAE (or Caution! Gang Warily)

by Peter Livingston, Dundee 1850

Tak time, my bonnie bairnie, dinna flee awa sae fast,
Never mind though 'mong your schoolmates you sometimes are the last;
It's not the hardest rinner that always gains the day,
Tak time, my bonnie bairn, and aye creep before you gae.
In the world's broad field of battle, when fechtin wi' the strife
And struggling hard for happiness and comfort in this life:
You'll find it aye the best way, when pulling up the brae,
Take time, my bonnie bairn, and aye creep before you gae.

The wisest man hath said, and what he says is rarely wrong,
The race is seldom to the swift, the battle to the strong;
The willing back has aft to bear the burthen o' the day,
Tak time, my bonnie bairn, and aye creep before you gae.
We have need to use, whilst here, all the caution that we can,
In playing at the game o' life wi' wily-hearted man;
The lion's heart — the eagle's eye — the fox's cunning way
Are wanted here, tak time, my bairn, creep before you gae.

132

Gentlemen — The Tartan

"Here's to it;
The fighting sheen of it;
The yellow, the green of it;
The white, the blue of it;
The dark, the red of it;
Every thread of it;
The fair have sighed for it;
The brave have died for it;
Foemen sought for it;
Honour the name of it;
Drink to the fame of it —
The Tartan!"

Old Scots Toast

Murdoch Maclean

T. A. Jardine
(Jardine Clan Tartan),
dark and light brown with blue and red

A. T. Jardine
(Pipe Major
of Fettes College Pipe Band 1980)

Proceeds from the sale of this edition will go to the Rescue Fund established by The Museum of Scottish Tartans, Comrie, Perthshire, to save unique items of Highland Dress for the Nation.
The Museum is a recognised Charity.

Readers may like to do further study on the History of the Largo area and Alexander Selkirk. Here then are some of the books I have found both useful and interesting.

SELECTED BIBLIOGRAPHY

"Guide to the East Neuk of Fife", 1886. D. Hay Fleming.
"History of the County of Fife", 1840. John Leighton.
"The Shores of Fife", 1872. William Ballingall.
"Fishing Boats and Fisher Folk on the East Coast of Scotland", 1930. Peter Anson.
"The East Neuk of Fife", 1887. Rev. Walter Wood.
"Flax and Linen in Fife through the Centuries", 1952. P. K. Livingstone.
"Fish and Fisheries, the Prize Essays of the International Fisheries Exhibition, Edinburgh", 1882. D. Herbit.
"Fife, Kinross & Clackmannan, The Royal Commission of Ancient and Historical Monuments of Scotland", 1930.
"Lamont's Diary, 1649-71".
"Robinson Crusoe's Island: a History of the Juan Fernandez Islands", 1969. Professor Ralf Lee Woodward, U.S.A.
"A British Privateer in the time of Queen Anne (The Story of Alexander Selkirk)", Robert C. Leslie.
"Cruising Voyage Round the World", 1712. Captain Woodes Rogers.
"Largo Village Book", 1932. Largo Women's Rural Institute.
"Statistical Account, Parish of Largo", 1791. Rev. Spence Oliphant.
J. Howell (1825) and R. L. Megroz (1936) books contain many inaccurate statements.

District Librarian, North East Fife District Council, Duncan Institute, Cupar, Fife.
Largo Parish Historian: William Reid, M.A., F.E.I.S., Lundin Links, Fife.

"An Island in Largo," a play written by the Fife playwright Sue Glover, had its world premiere in the Byre Theatre, St. Andrews, in October 1981. The play, about the life of Alexander Selkirk, was directed by Adrian Reynolds.
Chairman: A. B. Paterson, M.B.E.
Administrator: Jon Whatson.
Director of productions: Adrian Reynolds.

The Scottish Tartans Society, Museum of Scottish Tartans, Comrie, Perthshire.
    President: The Rt. Hon. The Earl of Elgin & Kincardine, D.L., J.P.
    Director & Secretary: Dr. Michiel McDonald.
    Chairman: Dr. Gordon Teall of Teallach.
    Co-ordinator of Research: Captain T. S. Davidson.

Jardine Clan Society.
    President: Colonel Sir William Jardine of Applegirth, Bt., O.B.E., T.D., D.L.,
    22nd Hereditary Chief of Clan Jardine, Denbie, Lockerbie, Dumfriesshire.
    Genealogical Secretary: Miss Violet Jardine, 33 Edderston Road, Peebles.
    Treasurer: Mr. A. Jardine, Spedline, 27 Terregles Street, Dumfries.
    Clan Piper: Allan T. Jardine, Cardy House, Lower Largo, Fife.

The Scottish Fisheries Museum, St. Ayles, Harbourhead, Anstruther, Fife KY10 3AB.

Kirkcaldy Museum & Art Galleries, Kirkcaldy, Fife.

The National Museum of Antiquities of Scotland, Queen Street, Edinburgh EH2 1JD.

Scottish Records Office, H.M. General Register House, P.O. Box 36, Edinburgh EH1 3YY.

Scots Ancestry Research Society, 3 Albany Street, Edinburgh EH1 3PY.

The Scottish Genealogical Society, 9 Union Street, Edinburgh EH1 3LT.

National Library of Scotland, George IV Bridge, Edinburgh.

Scottish Tourist Board, 23 Ravelston Terrace, Edinburgh EH4 3EU.